aperture

Eyes Open

23
Photography
Projects
for
Curious
Kids

by
Susan Meiselas

An Invitation

Susan Meiselas began her career photographing the kids in her neighborhood. She is known for collaborating with the people she photographs and their communities long after the pictures are made.

Carol, JoJo and Lisa hanging out on Broome Street, New York City, 1976

In this book, I invite you to explore the world through photography. The camera can be a way of connecting to people and places while also expressing yourself.

Here you can begin to think about how to focus, to frame, to see light, movement, and emotions, to see interactions, and to imagine beyond what's in front of you.

Each prompt points you on a path, starting with pictures by students from around the world and followed by the words and images of artists who share different ways of seeing.

You can
experience this
book in any order
you like.

Dip or dive in
as you turn
the pages and
begin your own
photographic
journey.

Susan Meiselas,
*Santa Claus on Fifth
Avenue, New York City*,
1976; from the series
Volunteers of America

23
Photography
Projects

01

Alphabetography

Imagine making your own alphabet. Can you find objects, lines, and forms that look like each letter?

Discover letters in natural and human-made structures, or in shadows, or make them by cropping with the frame of the camera.

9

Eleanor Kaminski,
New York City

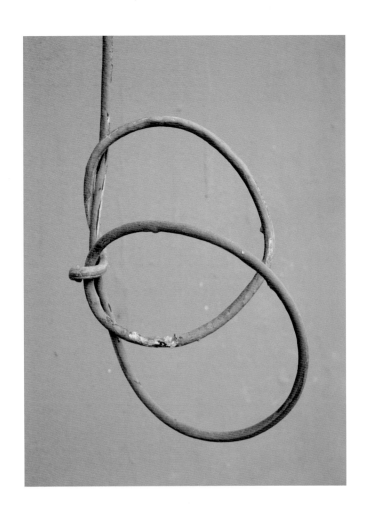

"A has gotten to Z
in the same order since the
Phoenicians designed it
that way, but these alphabets
prove how fluid and creative
letters and language can be.
The alphabet we learn as
law is, in fact, an ongoing act
of the imagination."
—Wendy Ewald

B brother n. & adj.
1) A fellow member of a group.
2) A person you know all about.

The brother in this picture
has his back turned.
—Tierra Lofton

Wendy Ewald
collaborates with children
around the world to
create alphabets that
reflect their communities.

B,
*An African American
Alphabet*, 2000

T talk v.i. & t.
To speak, to express
speech.

The boy is always
talking trash.
—Mark Stoves

Wendy Ewald, *T,*
An African American
Alphabet, 2000

X n.
Twenty-fourth letter
of the alphabet.

I'm entering the X-games.
—Jermaine Whiteside

Wendy Ewald, *X,*
An African American
Alphabet, 2000

02

Same but Different

How many types
of one thing can you find?

How are they the
same or different from
each other?

Emily Lee,
New York CIty

Same but Different

Top:
Ntwari Yan,
Gisenyi, Rwanda

Bottom:
Tuyisere Osama,
Gisenyi, Rwanda

Right:
Niyonzima Didier,
Gisenyi, Rwanda

19

Zoe Leonard uses
the form of typology,
photographing
many examples of the
same kind of thing,
to create a series.

Analogue, 1998–2009
(detail)

"Photography is always
tied to the real world. There's
an act of observation, but
it's not just recording what's
there. It's about framing
something and seeing it in
your own way. It's how you're
looking as much as what
you're looking at."
—Zoe Leonard

03
Reframe

Can you use lines and rectangles—like windows, doorways, and poles— to create a frame within the picture's frame?

What happens when you reframe something special you want to show?

Saul Leiter captured the life of New York City's streets, often experimenting with abstract compositions.

Through Boards, 1957

"I like it when one is not certain what one sees. When we do not know why the photographer has taken a picture and when we do not know why we are looking at it, all of a sudden we discover something that we start seeing."
—Saul Leiter

04

Light

Left:
KeSean Taylor-Jack,
New York City

Right:
William Murray,
Brooklyn

Can you capture how light shapes, hides, exaggerates, and transforms where and what it touches?

Rinko Kawauchi is known for capturing the extraordinary details within everyday life.

Untitled, 2011; from the series Illuminance

"I want imagination in the photographs I take. You wonder, 'What's going on?' You feel something is going to happen."
—Rinko Kawauchi

29

No matter where he travels, Alex Webb uses light and shadow to add layers in his pictures.

Nuevo Laredo, Mexico, 1996

India, 1981

"When I look at a scene, I am sensing not just what seems to be happening in front of my eyes and the various shapes that fill the frame, but I am also aware of . . . the color of light, the angle of light: how a shaft of light, or a particular tone of light, can utterly transform a situation."
—Alex Webb

05

Movement

Right:
Vanessa Hernandez,
Vista, California

Overleaf:
Elizabeth Avila,
New York City

How does the camera
capture motion in ways that
our eyes cannot?

Try to freeze action or
show the path of movement
through a long exposure.

"Sometimes people ask me, 'How many pictures do you take?' . . . Well, there is no rule. Sometimes, like this picture in Greece, I saw the frame of the whole thing, and I waited for somebody to pass. I snapped two pictures. . . . The little girl was exactly the thing in relation to the other shapes."
                    —Henri Cartier-Bresson

Henri Cartier-Bresson invented the term "decisive moment" to describe when all the elements of a scene line up in perfect harmony.

Siphnos, Greece, 1961

"All my images are made using long exposures, from a few seconds to an hour, and whatever available light is present at the scene. Much of photography is an attempt to stop the clock—to say, 'I was here.' My photographs are doing something different: we are shown the fleeting nature of our presence."
    —Matthew Pillsbury

Matthew Pillsbury explores how humans interact with different city environments by making pictures with long exposures, like this one from his book *City Stages*.

Dinosaur Comes to Life, American Museum of Natural History, New York, 2004

06
Animals Around You

When you see animals in the world around you, think about their state of being, their conditions, their habitat.

How do they live: enclosed, roaming, wild, domesticated?

Left:
Mamata Bom,
Surkhet, Nepal

Below:
Swastika Dhaulakoti,
Surkhet, Nepal

In his book *A*, Gregory Halpern photographed animals along with people, places, and landscapes, weaving a visual story.

Untitled, 2010

"Animals are like humans in the sense that they want and need the same basic things. But humans hide their feelings, whereas animals reveal fear, anger, and affection so readily."
—Gregory Halpern

For her book *Animals*, Sage Sohier looked at the lives of people intertwined with their pets, from llamas and pythons to house cats.

Girl with Rabbit and German Shepherd, Laconia, New Hampshire, 1992

Boy in Barn with Cat and Pony, Rowley, Massachusetts, 1992

"People are proud of their animals and like to show them off. Animals are active, funny, and surprising, so people tend to be much less self-conscious in front of the camera."
—Sage Sohier

07
Nature Study

Where does nature interact with the built environment?

How is it surviving in places you wouldn't expect to find it?

Left:
Kahri Griffin,
Brooklyn

Below:
Andrey Silva,
São Paulo, Brazil

Leslie Garcia Guzman,
Brooklyn

Frida Sofía Solano Morales,
Xalapa, Mexico

"Sociable weaverbirds take over the telephone poles that cut across their habitat. They collect twigs and grass to build these giant nests, which give strangely recognizable personalities to the man-made poles."
—Dillon Marsh

Dillon Marsh focuses on
the landscape of South Africa,
reflecting on how humans
and animals interact with it,
both purposefully and
unintentionally.

Assimilation, 2010

Robert Adams is known for his work in the vast landscape of the American West, portraying nature's beauty in contrast to destructive human forces.

Above the Elk River, Curry County, Oregon, 1999–2003

"If you get close to a clear-cut, where a forest is cut down, you're reminded of a battle scene. Everything is torn to pieces. My pictures of these places are a mixture of some-thing close to despair and a desperate attempt to find a basis for hope."
                    —Robert Adams

53

08
Neighborhood

What gives your neighbor-
hood a distinct character?

Can you find the details
which reveal what's
particular about the place
where you live?

Right and overleaf:
Maria E. Romero Gomez,
Los Angeles

Devin Allen focuses on his hometown, documenting both ordinary life and lives interrupted by dramatic events.

Untitled, 2015; from the book *A Beautiful Ghetto*, 2015

"I just wanted to show the world the Baltimore that I knew. I wanted to talk about the cookout, the block party. I wanted to show the resilience of the people. For so long, we allowed outsiders to tell our stories. The goal is to reclaim the story of our community."
—Devin Allen

In his book *House Hunting*, Todd Hido photographed typical American houses at night, giving the viewer just enough detail to imagine the life within.

#2690, 2000

"Most of the time, I am interested in a certain light in a window—that's what catches my attention. When you're looking at a house at night with its lights on, you can't help but imagine the people inside. In a strange way, I'm making a picture of a place that's actually about people."
—Todd Hido

61

09

Personal Space

How does a room express the personalities of those who live there?

Left:
Kayceeny Campbell,
Chiapas, Mexico

Below:
Talia Santiago,
Chiapas, Mexico

Below:
Kate Ruwe, Hampstead,
North Carolina

Right:
Abbey Ellerglick,
Charlottesville, Virginia

65

"When I'm in someone else's house—what kind of books do they have? What are they reading? It's just another way to try to glean who this person is. What's going on inside of them? We only have so many clues. We see how people dress. We see their mannerisms. And an interior provides all of this other information."
    —Alec Soth

Alec Soth sometimes
starts with a list of ideas
or scenes to photograph.
Then the pictures lead
him from one to the next
until there are enough
to create a book, such as
Dog Days Bogotá.

*Untitled 36, Bogotá,
Colombia*, 2003

In his book *Project Family*, Motoyuki Daifu gives an inside look at his family life within a small apartment in Yokohama, Japan.

Untitled, 2010–17; from *Project Family*

"I have a relationship to the space that no one else has. There's something there that only I can photograph. I think maybe it's better to take a place I know and get to know it better."
—Motoyuki Daifu

10
Strangers Met

Think about all the people you encounter every day but don't really know.

Can you ask to portray them where you see them most often?

Left:
Emily Paravaris,
Caracas, Venezuela

Below:
Alexis Castro,
Brooklyn

"These photos are all shot from the position of a person entering the office, with the desk in between. And they are square because that is the most boring format and so the most appropriate for a dull subject, like govern-ment offices. Even so, the pictures are full of telling details: some that reveal the way different officials express their power, some that show a more private character."

—Jan Banning

Jan Banning
photographed hundreds
of officials from eight
countries on five
continents, creating a
comparative study for his
book *Bureaucratics*.

*Russia, Bureaucracy,
Siberia, Province Tomsk*,
2004

73

Jan Banning
Clockwise from top left:

*China, Bureaucracy,
Shandong*, 2005

*India, Bureaucracy,
Bihar*, 2004

*USA, Bureaucracy,
Texas*, 2007

Yemen, Bureaucracy,
2007

Clockwise from top left:

*Bolivia, Bureaucracy
(police), Potosi*, 2005

*France, Bureaucracy,
Auvergne*, 2006

Liberia, Bureaucracy,
2006

Liberia, Bureaucracy,
2006

Nikki S. Lee places herself with different identity groups in her pictures to play with ideas of how we view others and ourselves.

The Tourist Project (9), 1997

The Punk Project (1), 1997

"I transformed myself into different types of people and took snapshots with them. I realized I couldn't understand who I am without the people around me. I believe that it is only through my relationships with others that I can see myself."
—Nikki S. Lee

11
Portraits in a Place

Can you place yourself in a landscape that is meaningful to you?

Left:
Francis Lozeau,
Pablo, Montana

Right:
Colin Yuan,
Los Angeles

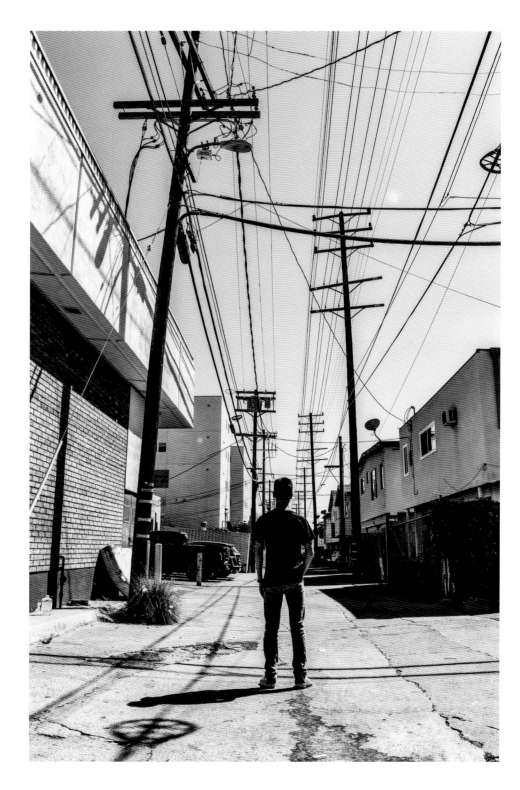

"Photography for me is just
an excuse to get to know
the world. When you are an
artist or a photographer,
you always need to establish
a connection to the place
where you are. Without the
camera, you see the world
one way; with it, you see the
world another way."
—Graciela Iturbide

Graciela Iturbide is best
known for her poetic
portrayal of life and the
landscape in her home
country, Mexico.

*Self Portrait, Botanic
Garden, Oaxaca*, 1999

12
Portraits in Disguise

Can you make
a portrait that gives
a sense of the person
without showing
their face?

Left:
Shawn Gardner,
Dayton, Ohio

Below:
Ajaya Shelton,
Dayton, Ohio

"We played at picture-
making, using their bodies
and objects found around
the building as content,
and using this environment
as a stage for imagining
something beyond it.
The images themselves also
play with revealing and
obscuring."
　　　—Carolyn Drake

Carolyn Drake collaborated with girls in a Ukrainian orphanage on the edge of a forest to explore imaginative expressions of themselves.

Ternopil, Petrykhiv, 2016; from the series Internat

13

People I Know

Can you make a portrait of a friend that reveals their more private, rather than public, self?

Left:
Criselda Mele,
Los Angeles

Right:
Alessia Hu,
New York City

Dawoud Bey breaks the tradition of choosing one picture as the portrait of a person by juxtaposing different moments together.

Aurora, Andover, Massachusetts, 1993

"I believe there is an interesting story to every person. The challenge is how to make that visible. Merely pointing the camera at a person is not going to do it. I'm looking for the way inner thoughts and feelings make themselves visible on the face and body. This reveals a sense of the whole living, breathing person."
—Dawoud Bey

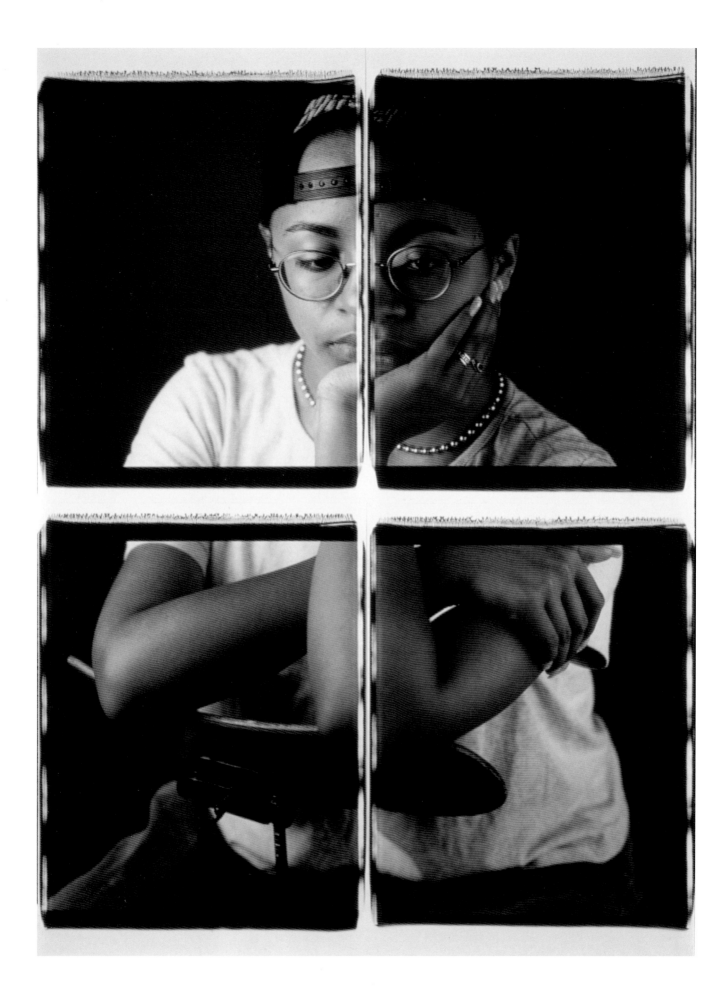

89

14
Family

Observe your family just being themselves.

Can you capture them when they're not posing or thinking about how they look for the camera?

Left and below:
Genesis Harris, New York City

Ana Edwards,
New York City

93

Nada Louisse,
Paris

For her book *Immediate Family*, Sally Mann collaborated with her three children at their summer home in Virginia, making pictures that form an extended family portrait.

Sorry Game, 1989

"The place is important; the time is summer. It's any summer, but the place is home and the people here are my family. . . . Many of these pictures are intimate, some are fictions and some are fantastic, but most are of ordinary things every mother has seen."
—Sally Mann

For his series The House
That Bleeds, Yael Martínez
photographed his family
to trace a personal journey
through loss.

The House That Bleeds,
2013

The Dark Root, 2012

"I might not be able to
travel to the other side of the
world, but there are very
important stories that need
to be told right here, where
I am. This is why I decided
to portray my own family and
community—showing
the aspects that go unseen."
—Yael Martínez

15
Me

Leslie Garcia   Ms.136

I am from coldness and chocolate sweet ice cream in cold stone and bamboo that my dad brings home because he thinks it's pretty also my whole family looks alike and wears glasses. Also in my house I speak Spanish because my parents and big brother are from Mexico but in school I have to speak English.

Can you share a story about yourself that goes with and beyond what the picture shows?

Leslie Garcia Guzman,
Brooklyn

my name is Natalie, I have 8 yearsold
I Love to swim and Play with my 3
sibilings. I have an immigiant
fameily my mom is from Guatzmalan
and my dady is from Mexico.
we live in New york

My Home

Natalie Rodrigúez,
New York City

Me llamo kevin soy de Mexico
tengo uno familia imigrante.

y yo crose la frontera.

a mime gustan los video Juegos
yo tengo un hermano y hermana.
y hablo mixteco que es una lengua
indigena

Kevin Diego,
New York City

"My name is Kevin and I'm from
an immigrant family from Mexico.
I like to play video games with
my brother and sister. I speak
Mixteco which is a local language."

Jim Goldberg often
asks the people in his
photographs to add their
stories to his pictures,
as he did in San Francisco
with his book *Rich
and Poor*.

*Sharon D. Butts,
San Francisco, California,
1979*

"A lot of photographs are taken from the outside looking in. And I was interested in something else—letting people describe experiences in their own words, from the inside, with pictures that sometimes went with, and sometimes went against, what they were saying."
—Jim Goldberg

What I really want is a real home ~~toth~~ with nice furniture, also a van to drive. I also would like to give my son ~~oat~~ what I didn't get in life. Which includes love.

Sharon D. Butts

Writing on historical images of her Crow ancestors, Wendy Red Star adds an alternative view about the people and culture to make them more visible.

Long Horse, Sits in the Middle of the Land, and White Calf, 2017

"Even though I grew up in the community and on the reservation, this is how I'm learning more about my heritage. I'm patching pieces of our historical timeline back together as a way of archiving the culture and history of my people, which are not widely known."
—Wendy Red Star

16
Generations

Susana Petrona Pérez
de la Torre,
Chiapas, Mexico

Can you remember or
portray someone in your
family from a different
generation?

"My grandmother played a central role in my life; her oral histories and the lessons she instilled in me fueled my desire to fly further than I was allowed to go."

Reverse, not shown: "They said, 'Women don't have any right to talk, but only to receive orders and follow them,' because for many, a woman continues to be just a basket without a voice, without a soul, without life."

Mi abuela desempeñó un papel medular en mi vida, porque gracias a sus historias contadas y aprendizajes inculcados en mí, han hecho que yo quiera volar más allá de lo permitido.

Susana Petrona Pérez
de la Torre,
Chiapas, Mexico

"We're all connected intergenerationally—we're connected to the images of the past and to the future. I'm thinking about time travel when I make my work—take, as an example, my work with my mother and my grand-mother. I'm suggesting we are one entity; we are all markers on a timeline that is cyclical."

—LaToya Ruby Frazier

In *The Notion of Family*,
LaToya Ruby Frazier
photographs three
generations of her family
as part of the larger
story of her hometown's
decline.

Grandma Ruby and Me,
2005

17
Parallel Lives

Alana Thaynara,
São Paulo, Brazil

Can you recreate a family picture—thinking about the setting, gestures, and expressions—and imagine yourself in a family member's past life?

Gabriela Rodriguez,
New York City

Kaylee Brown,
New York City

Looking at old photo-
graphs of her mother and
then finding the clothes
she was wearing inspired
Lebohang Kganye to
make the series Ke Lefa
Laka: Her-story.

*Habo Patience
ka Bokhathe II*, 2013

"I would dress in the exact clothes
that she was wearing in these
twenty-year-old photographs
and mimic the same poses.
This was my way of marrying the
two memories (mine and
my mother's) to reconstruct
a new story."
　　　—Lebohang Kganye

18

Now & Then

Eighth Avenue Station,
ca. 1960; from the Brooklyn
Historical Society

Can you find an old picture of someplace near where you live and go back to see what it looks like now?

Lilian Recinos Sola,
Brooklyn

In *Reconstructing the View*, Mark Klett and Byron Wolfe photograph the Grand Canyon, stitching their images together with iconic pictures of the same view.

Woman on Head and Photographer with Camera; Unknown Dancer and Alvin Langdon Coburn at Grand View Point, 2009

"We call them mash-ups of different times, experiences, and ways of looking at the place. We respond to how a place has been photographed before, looking for what's changed, what connections can be made."
—Mark Klett and Byron Wolfe

Shimon Attie projects images from the past onto today's cities. *The History of Another* shows modern-day Rome with pictures of Roman Jews from the 1900s.

On Via della Tribuna di Campitelli, Rome, Italy, 2003. On-location slide projection

"I think of my work as a kind of peeling back of the wallpaper of today to reveal the histories buried underneath."
—Shimon Attie

19
Icons

Can you find a famous painting and place yourself in it?

Left:
Johannes Vermeer,
The Milkmaid, 1660

Below:
Matías Vicente Antonio
Diego, Guatemala City

Pablo Picasso,
Absinthe Drinker, 1901

Francisco Diego,
Guatemala City

Cindy Sherman dresses
up and photographs
herself as different
imagined characters
in various situations,
including iconic paintings.

Untitled #224, 1990

"I'm good at using my face as a canvas. . . . I'll see a photograph of a character and try to copy them onto my face. I think I'm really observant— thinking about how a person is put together . . . and noticing subtle things about them that make them who they are."
—Cindy Sherman

129

20

Double Exposure

Right:
Aubrey Sierra,
Vista, California

Overleaf:
Leslie Cervantes,
Vista, California

Can you show multiple
realities or different moods
by experimenting
with double exposure?

130

"It was the worst ten years
    of my life. I was away from
    my family from the age
    of six to sixteen. How do
    you learn about family? I
    didn't know what love was.
    We weren't even known
    by names back then. I was
    a number."
"Do you remember your
    number?"
"73."

"Double exposures allow for an extra layer of storytelling. My project about First Nations people who were forced to go to boarding school as children, where they were not allowed to speak their own languages, combines portraits with the sites and memories of their experiences. To me, a straight portrait wasn't going to be enough to tell that story."
—Daniella Zalcman

In her series Signs of Your Identity, Daniella Zalcman combines two or more pictures together, embedding history within her portrayal of Indigenous survivors.

Mike Pinay, Qu'Appelle Indian Residential School, 1953–1963, 2015

21

People Puzzles

Can you make one face or body from multiple pictures of your friends to create a new identity?

Ada Chen,
New York City

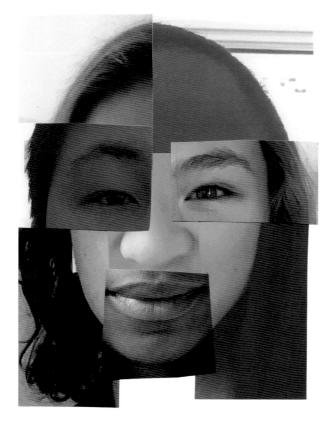

Left:
Kylie Lough,
Andover,
Massachusetts

Right:
Ruby Sabir,
Toronto

Daniel Gordon cuts up photographs and other materials to create three-dimensional objects that he photographs into portraits.

Crescent Eyed Portrait, 2012

"I was interested in what happened if I took out the identifiable parts of a face. How far could I push the idea of a portrait? How far could I go away from what an eye is, or what a nose is, or what a mouth is, and still hopefully have it read as a portrait in some way." —Daniel Gordon

22

Collage

Can you create
an imaginary world
for yourself?

Left:
Nevaeh Mills,
Queens, New York

Above:
Natalie Rodrigúez,
New York City

Kevin Diego,
New York City

Michel Guadalupe Animas,
New York City

In her collages, Mickalene Thomas portrays Black women posed confidently among patterns and surfaces often found in the home.

Din avec la main dans le miroir, 2008

"It's making sense of all these things that are in your everyday life. . . . You take all of the components and you make it into your own— sourcing very various cultural, metaphorical, and spiritual aspects, and combining them together, which is collage."
—Mickalene Thomas

147

23

Imagined Landscapes

Below:
Emily Martin,
Eeyou Istchee, Canada

Right:
Samantha Rupert,
Eeyou Istchee, Canada

Can you add something beyond the surface of what you see in a photograph to show what's missing or invisible?

"When we look around us, the
past appears to be invisible, but
it is always present. For me,
memory is memory; whether
personal or historical, it is
the same. Through making art,
I give voice to these invisible
narratives."
　　　—Clarissa Sligh

Cherry Blossoms across the Tidal Basin, Washington, D. C.

In her series Reframing the Past, Clarissa Sligh visualizes a larger history by combining text and images with materials from her family album.

Cherry Blossoms, 1984

In Closing

Photography is a collaboration between you and the people you are photographing. Together you participate in the making of the picture.

When you point your camera at a person, a place, or a community, think about what you want to convey. Who is the picture for? The people in the picture? Yourself? Or both? What are you sharing? What are you giving back? This is what I always ask myself.

Whether or not a photograph can change the world, photography can change you.

Just open your eyes!

ALPHABETOGRAPHY

The student locates objects, lines and forms which most resemble each letter of the alphabet, from A to Z. Letters can be discovered in natural and man-made forms, found in shadows, or made by cropping with the frame of the camera.

1

Susan Meiselas
Riverview Elementary School ▲
Fort Mill, S. Carolina

ANY OLD ALPHABET

Each child or small group chooses a subject, such as toys or food, and then proceeds to find and photograph objects that begin with each letter of the alphabet.

2

Toys
a
b
c

Joan Stevenson
Catawba Academy ●
Rock Hill, S. Carolina
Photographs by Neal Stevenson

PERSONAL SPACE

The reason for taking these pictures was to give importance to objects that are familiar, but rarely singled out. To look at all objects from their normal, everyday perspectives helps the elderly get used to the camera as an extension of themselves. This gives their environment, their own personal space, and their lives more significance. Photographic recordings become a legacy to pass on.

58

Theresa Craddock / Susan Piechote
Boston Center for Older Americans ★
Boston, Mass.
Photographs by Hazel Danaby

PHOTO ESSAY: NORTH WEST RIVER, LABRADOR

59

"I like to take pictures because it is fun to take or keep for a long time. It also can let you remember where, who, and what it is like. I took these pictures because I know what I feel about them and I feel so bad because most of the people who work at the sawmill are not paid as the people over across the river. Some people have to walk all the way down the hill just to get some water, the pump houses they made are not good. The garbage is not sent away to another place where there is nobody instead of lying on the ground. At the school only grade IX course is being done there. If grade XI was being done there it would be better. The garden there in the picture is a potato garden which is not very good. It is used for the people who don't have enough money to buy potatoes in the store."

Wendy Ewald
North West River ■
Labrador
Photographs by Benedict Michel

The Story of This Book

I began my own journey as an image-maker nearly fifty years ago, teaching photography in elementary schools in the South Bronx, and later in South Carolina and Mississippi. At that time, I saw the camera as a way to expand the boundaries of the classroom.

I taught making and interpreting images as a kind of visual reading and writing. The kids would go out to make photos of whatever caught their interest—somebody's car or the butcher shop. We'd come back together, and they'd show their pictures. Each time, I'd ask, "So why did you take that picture?" We'd try to figure out what was in the photograph that had drawn them to make it. Each time, this process of discovery led to a story.

Today, photography surrounds us far beyond the classroom. Everybody can be an image-maker now in a way that we couldn't have imagined decades ago when there were no camera phones. Then, we made pinhole cameras out of shoeboxes, processed pictures in a darkroom, and used Polaroid cameras with instant film. Polaroid was magical, and the instant photograph shaped what was possible. Instead of having to teach how to make a print, we could focus on what a photograph is.

After a few years of working in schools, I contacted over one hundred teachers who were using photography to participate in *Learn to See*, a sourcebook of ideas from and for teachers and students, published by the Polaroid Foundation in 1974.

Eyes Open has a similar approach. This time with Aperture, we reached out to an extensive network of teachers from around the world. They shared their ideas and the work of their students. Complementing those contributions, we selected artists whose visions—through images and words—expand a visual language. This was a collective effort to inspire image-makers to create ongoing exchanges and explore visual dialogues across generations.

I am especially grateful to all the students, teachers, and artists who generously participated in the making of this visual reader. There have been many eyes and hands involved in this process. I want to thank the Aperture team: Charlotte Chudy, who put a system in place for wide outreach; Bowen Fernie and Joanna Knutsen, who launched our call to a network of teachers; and Lanah Swindle, who masterfully managed the research, multiple tasks of revisions, and permissions. Thanks to both Alexis Lambrou and Alice Proujansky, who were valuable thought-partners in the early stages, focusing on who this book might best serve. I am appreciative of Alex Nelson, Sumeja Tulic, Luciana Pinchiero, and Jessica Bal from my Mott Street studio, who were always encouraging, as well as my sister, Nancy Berner, whose support gave me perspective as the book took shape.

Most especially, I am grateful to Denise Wolff, who week by week, and over multiple years, remained an exceptionally dedicated editor, collaborating and adapting as our concept evolved. Her steady hand and eye made this book possible.

Credits

We are grateful to the following teachers, who submitted the student images in this book:

—

01 Alphabetography:
Jessica Sinclair, Lower Manhattan Community Middle School, New York; Dolores Medel, Universidad Veracruzana Extension, Xalapa, Mexico

02 Same but Different:
Lisa Stancati, William A. Shine Great Neck South High School, Great Neck, New York; Jean Bizimana, Kristen Ashburn, Gadi Habumugisha, and Mussa Uwitonze, Through the Eyes of Children, Gisenyi, Rwanda

03 Reframe:
Original concept and work submitted by Lisa Stancati, William A. Shine Great Neck South High School, Great Neck, New York; additional work submitted by Lisa DiFilippo, Millennium High School, New York

04 Light:
Alexis Lambrou, NYC Salt, New York; Alice Proujansky, Aperture On Sight, Brooklyn

05 Movement:
Kelly Clark, Rancho Buena Vista High School, Vista, California; Emily Schiffer, NYC Salt, New York

06 Animals Around You:
Kristen Ashburn, Jean Bizimana, Gadi Habumugisha, and Mussa Uwitonze, Through the Eyes of Children and BlinkNow, Surkhet, Nepal

07 Nature Study:
Hugo Rojas, Reel Works, Mott Hall Bridges Academy, Brooklyn; João Kulcsár, Alfabetização Visual, São Paulo, Brazil; Gordon Baldwin and Alice Proujansky, Aperture On Sight, Charles O. Dewey Middle School 136, Brooklyn; Dolores Medel, Universidad Veracruzana Extension, Xalapa, Mexico

08 Neighborhood:
Arlene Mejorado, Las Fotos Project, Los Angeles

09 Personal Space:
Lou Dembrow and Lyn Pentecost, The Lower Eastside Girls Club, New York, and Archivo Fotográfico Indígena, Chiapas, Mexico

10 Strangers Met:
Lexi Parra and Diko Betancourt, Project MiRa, Caracas, Venezuela; Gordon Baldwin and Alice Proujansky, Aperture On Sight, Charles O. Dewey Middle School 136, Brooklyn

11 Portraits in a Place:
Leah Stahl, Stivers School for the Arts, Dayton, Ohio

12 Portraits in Disguise:
Joe Medina, Harvard-Westlake School, Los Angeles; Emily Schiffer, NYC Salt, New York

13 People I Know:
Original concept and work submitted by David J. Spear, A VOICE—Art Vision & Outreach in Community Education, Our Community Record project in collaboration with Two Eagle River School, Flathead Nation, Pablo, Montana; additional work submitted by Joe Medina, Harvard-Westlake School, Los Angeles

14 Family:
Ben Russell, High School of Fashion Industries, New York; Anita Pouchard Serra, Parole de photographes, École élémentaire Philippe de Girard, Paris

15 Me:
Gordon Baldwin and Alice Proujansky, Aperture On Sight, Charles O. Dewey Middle School 136, Brooklyn; Cinthya Santos-Briones, Transnational Villages Network/Red de Pueblos Transnacionales (RPT), New York

16 Generations:
Maya Goded, Stsebetik Bolom ("Jaguar's Daughters"), Chiapas, Mexico

17 Parallel Lives:
Original concept and work submitted by Destiny Mata, The Lower Eastside Girls Club, New York; additional work submitted by João Kulcsár, Alfabetização Visual, São Paulo, Brazil

18 Now & Then:
Gordon Baldwin and Alice Proujansky, Aperture On Sight, Charles O. Dewey Middle School 136, Brooklyn

19 Icons:
Original concept and work submitted by Rocío Auyón, Fotokids, Guatemala City

20 Double Exposure:
Kelly Clark, Rancho Buena Vista High School, Vista, California

21 People Puzzles:
Diana Nazareth, Project Kids & Cameras, Toronto; Hector René Membreno-Canales, Phillips Academy, Andover, Massachusetts; Jessica Sinclair, Lower Manhattan Community Middle School, New York

22 Collage:
Sol Aramendi, The Bellaire School PS 135Q, CASA program in partnership with the Queens Museum; Cinthya Santos-Briones, Transnational Villages Network/Red de Pueblos Transnacionales (RPT), New York

23 Imagined Landscapes:
Original concept and work submitted by Hannah Doucet, Helen Moore, and Nalakwsis, Mikw Chiyâm Program, Eeyou Istchee, Quebec, Canada

We are grateful to the students and artists who participate as authors in this book through their images and words:

—

Students:
Elizabeth Avila, Mamata Bom, Kaylee Brown, Kayceeny Campbell, Alexis Castro, Leslie Cervantes, Ada Chen, Swastika Dhaulakoti, Francisco Diego, Kevin Diego, Matías Vicente Antonio Diego, Ana Edwards, Abbey Ellerglick, Leslie Garcia Guzman, Shawn Gardner, Kahri Griffin, Michel Guadalupe Animas, Genesis Harris, Vanessa Hernandez, Alessia Hu, Eleanor Kaminski, Emily Lee, Kylie Lough, Nada Louisse, Francis Lozeau, Emily Martin, Criselda Mele, Nevaeh Mills, William Murray, Niyonzima Didier, Ntwari Yan, Emily Paravaris, Susana Petrona Pérez de la Torre, Lilian Recinos Sola, Gabriela Rodriguez, Natalie Rodríguez, Maria E. Romero Gomez, Hui Qiong Rong, Samantha Rupert, Kate Ruwe, Ruby Sabir, Talia Santiago, Ajaya Shelton, Aubrey Sierra, Andrey Silva, Frida Sofía Solano Morales, KeSean Taylor-Jack, Alana Thaynara, Tuyisere Osama, Jonathan Wong, Colin Yuan

Artists:
Robert Adams, Devin Allen, Shimon Attie, Jan Banning, Dawoud Bey, Henri Cartier-Bresson, Motoyuki Daifu, Carolyn Drake, Wendy Ewald, LaToya Ruby Frazier, Jim Goldberg, Daniel Gordon, Gregory Halpern, Todd Hido, Graciela Iturbide, Rinko Kawauchi, Lebohang Kganye, Mark Klett and Byron Wolfe, Nikki S. Lee, Saul Leiter, Zoe Leonard, Sally Mann, Dillon Marsh, Yael Martínez, Matthew Pillsbury, Wendy Red Star, Cindy Sherman, Clarissa Sligh, Sage Sohier, Alec Soth, Mickalene Thomas, Alex Webb, Daniella Zalcman

We are grateful to the following teachers and students, whose participation helped shape this project:

—

A VOICE—Art Vision & Outreach in Community Education, Our Community Record project in collaboration with Two Eagle River School, Flathead Nation, Pablo, Montana
Teacher: David J. Spear
Students: Frankie Barnaby, Michael Bolen, Josh Crumley, Francis Lozeau, Andy McDonald, Brittany Morigeau, Eneasa Pierre, Javyn Porter

Alfabetização Visual, São Paulo, Brazil
Teacher: João Kulcsár
Students: Giam Almeida, Ivan Anderson Campos, Claudio Augusto, Angelo Batistelli, Asir Ferreira Lopes, Alice Flor, Caio S. Furtado, Paulo Gustavo, Lucas Lima, Paola Lima, Rogerio Machado, Patricia Medrado, Felipe Monteiro Alves, Kedma Morena, Francisco Nascimento, Edvaldo Nascimento e Silva, Mariana Pereira, Gederson Pereira Bastos, Anderson Queiroz, Everton Ricardo, Vinicius Rocha Azevedo, Matheus Salvio, Vanessa Santanna, Amanda R. Silva, Ana Beatriz Silva, Andrey Silva, Stefany Silva, Geraldo Siqueira, Liniker Soares, Beatriz Souza, Edmar Tadashi, Katia Teixeira Ramos, Alana Thaynara, Nicole Vitoria

Arno Mkrtchyan Basic School, Hin Shen Village, Shoushi, Nagorno-Karabakh
Teacher: Sona Gevorgyan
Students: Angelina Grigoryan, Anoush Grigoryan, Mher Hovsepyan, Yuliana Hovsepyan, Marie Knyazyan, Aleksan Petrosov, Anna Petrosova, Grigori Sargsyan, Narek Taranyan, Vahe Taranyan

Art City, Winnipeg, Manitoba, Canada
Teacher: Natalie Baird
Students: 2018 film and photography students participated as a group

Bard High School Early College Manhattan, New York
Teacher: Alexis Lambrou
Students: Sally Rogers, Maya Silver

Bronx Documentary Center, New York
Teacher: Kamal Badhey
Teaching Assistants: Salvador Espinoza, Sean Sirota
Education Manager: Bianca Farrow
Students: Justin Arroyo, Justin Brefo, Heidi Calderon, Brandon Carchipulla, Raymond Castillo, Ivette Diaz Espinosa, Serenity Gomez, Sophia Morales, Leonely Pacheco, Tara Smalls, Dylan Velez, Kalise Williams

Teacher: Groana Melendez
Teaching Assistants: Monica Flores, Carla Rice, Jon Santiago
Education Manager: Bianca Farrow
Students: Fanny Aucacama, Jai Bhagwan, Izaiah Cardona, Darolin Cruz, Awa Fofana

Buxton School, Williamstown, Massachusetts
Teacher: Ben Ripley
Student: Tallula Sorst

CASA program, The Bellaire School PS 135Q, in partnership with the Queens Museum, New York
Teacher: Sol Aramendi
Students: Nazeeha Ahmed, Sehlyn Marie Alcotas, Ibnat Ashif Isha, Denisse Guaman, Dhruv Hazari, Alisha Hussain, Isabel Khuldiph, Dahlia Michaud, Nevaeh Mills, Nabil Mohammed, Faiza Nublat, Kiara Ramoutar, Rafidan Sauda

Charles O. Dewey Middle School 136, Brooklyn, in partnership with Aperture On Sight
Teachers: Gordon Baldwin, Alice Proujansky
Students: Adrian Acosta, Crystal Adames, Dariela Agusto, Laura Alba, Laith Alshugaa, Brenda Amacende Medina, Joselyn Ayachipo, Ruby Bonilla, Anais Cabrera, Crystal Carrion, Lizbeth Castillo Morales, Alexis Castro, Christopher Flores, Leslie Garcia Guzman, Tamara Guaman, Maria Gutierrez, Rachel Interiano, Theodore Isaiah, Karla V. Lopez, Tulio Lucas, Yasmin Luna, Fabiola Martinez, Tiara Mia Mercedes, Ailyn Mundo, Jose Onofre, Lizbeth Ramirez, Melvin Recio, Vincent Ren, Mariah Rodriguez, Emily Salem, Salameh Salem, Adriana San Lui, Jennifer Sarmiento, Silvia Sibrian, Lilian Recinos Sola, Henry Susquitana, Brandon Vasquez, Monte Vicente, Damaris Walker

Children and the Experience of Illness, Center for Documentary Studies, Duke University, Durham, North Carolina
Teacher: John Moses
Student: Melissa Rodriguez

Christina Noble Children's Foundation, Blue Skies Ger Village, Ulaanbaatar, Mongolia
Teacher: Amaraa Bor
Students: Odonchimeg Adiyasuren, Shinechimeg Adiyasuren, Namuundari Batsaikhan, Togtokh Battsetseg, Natalie Bauerova, Zoljargal Bold-Erdene, Yanjinlham Lhagvasuren, Suvd Narnaa, A. Nomin, Surdaa

Expanding the Walls, Studio Museum in Harlem, New York
Teacher: Ginny Huo
Students: Belen Vanesa Bautista, Charles Etuk, Bryam Franco, Leila Annah Fuentes, Aisha Hashmi, Steeve Hedouville, Emmanuel Lugo, Skye Mayo, David Mills, Michelle Morocho, Kenny Peña, Saiida Powell, Ashley Teague, Anthony Trowner, Sadia Zaman

Fotokids, Guatemala City
Teacher: Rocío Auyón
Founder: Nancy McGirr
Students: Josue Armando Mojiach, Santiago Canastuj, Alexander Chajón, Francisco Diego, Matías Vicente Antonio Diego, Andy García, Erick Hernández, Emelyn Mejía, Raúl Morales, Carlos Urbina, Odilia Vásquez

FotoKonbit, John F. Kennedy Middle School, North Miami Beach
Teacher: Tatiana Mora Liautaud
Students: Princy Alionice, Chrismaya Dorlean, Tyreka Dorlean, Christ Etienne, Christian Lucas, Jean Lucas

George School, Newtown, Pennsylvania
Teacher: Danielle Picard-Sheehan
Students: Jacob Bright, Mallory Fritsch, Nora Greer, Madeline Neway, Emma G. Schneider

Harvard-Westlake School, Los Angeles
Teacher: Joe Medina
Students: Anna Baron, Drew Bowser, Cynthia Camargo, Vivian Casas, Caitlin Chung, Georgia Gerber, Skylar Graham, Pablo Greenlee, Penelope Alexa Juarez, Abe Kaye, James Lassiter, Brody Listen, Criselda Mele, Kate von Mende, Cate Mittweg, Violet Morgan, Lauren Nehorai, Izzy Reif, Drew Roman, Mia Shelton, Sarina Smolev, Victoria Steckel, Caroline Sturgeon, Grace Swift, Vince Temesevary, Michael Vigman, Colin Yuan, Annabel Zimmer

High School of Art and Design, New York
Teacher: Brenna McLaughlin
Students: Natalia Alegarbes, Abigail Lugo, Jose Manosalvas, Kelly Rosas, Zoe Saintval, Jessica Sevillano

High School of Fashion Industries, New York
Teacher: Ben Russell
Students: Nysia Brown, Ashley Buela, Jane Choe, Ana Edwards, John Edwards, Nayeli Garcia, Genesis Harris, Sumona Lubna, Mia Minaya, Tatiana Rodriguez

Humanitas Academy of Art & Technology, Los Angeles
Teacher: Adriana Yugovich
Students: Stacey Garcia, Leilani Gonzalez, Fabiola Lopez, Yvette Muñoz, Sandra Sanchez, Cindy Torres, Ivan Zamora

International School of Florence, Italy
Teacher: Antoinette Blain
Students: Anna Cervini, Remy Chessell, Avery Fernie, Coco Li, Denzel Martinez, Jack Wang

Josephine Herrick Project, New York
Teacher: Diane Bezucha
Students: Shania Bynum, Sydni Carr, Emily Chen, Emanuel Foster, Comari Jenkins, Ada Jiang, Wendy Lei, Yatsing Lei, Ethan Pai, Michael Silva, Dasah Williams, Crystal Zheng, Fanny Zheng

Lamar Middle School and Fine Arts Academy, Austin, Texas
Teacher: Virginia Rowland
Students: Josie Blackwell, Sophia Dawson, Sophie Evans, Meredith Grotevant, Eliza Jensen, Gerald Jones, Alena Marquez, Eisele Mosby, Kylie Reeves, Thomas Ross, Pedro Sanchez, Hillary Stephens, Miles Whitehill, Andrew Wilson

Las Fotos Project, Los Angeles
Teacher: Arlene Mejorado
Students: Gabriela Acosta, Sofia Yan Araujo, Azul Covarrubias, Xochtil Q. Cruz, Athziri Flores, Andrea Popoca, Maria E. Romero Gomez, Celeste Umana

The Lower Eastside Girls Club, New York, and Archivo Fotográfico Indígena, Chiapas, Mexico
Teachers: Lou Dembrow, Lyn Pentecost
Students: Kayceeny Campbell, Talia Santiago

The Lower Eastside Girls Club, New York
Teacher: Destiny Mata
Students: Elaina Berman, Kaylee Brown, Lyannah Chiquito, Wisdom Dewberry, Sienna Garcia-Irizarry, Gabriela Rodriguez

Lower Manhattan Community Middle School, New York
Teacher: Jessica Sinclair
Students: Ada Chen, Rome Dimmick, Esther Feldsher, Daniel He, Eleanor Kaminski, Jasmine McAdams, Lisa Zeng

Manchester Craftsmen's Guild Photography, Pittsburgh
Teacher: Germaine Watkins
Students: Destiny Anderson, Ian Badke, Janae Bandy, Brandon Bennett, Cassie Csokuly, Aron Davenport, Zachary Lord, Dashia Mackewich, Josh Pratt, Anupama Rai, Christian Ray, Gustustano Rayes, Tyreek Scott, James Smith, Josh Walburn, Shaw Younger

Mikw Chiyâm Program, Eeyou Istchee, Quebec, Canada
Teachers: Hannah Doucet, Helen Moore, Nalakwsis
Students: Kaydie Dick, Rain Iserhoff, Khaydence Kawapit, Emily Martin, Angel Rupert, Samantha Rupert

Millennium High School, New York
Teacher: Lisa DiFilippo
Students: Christian Agosto, Mason Andriola, Nerma Bektesevic, Lillian Brown, Sara Bucior, Khanso Diawara, Fei Fei Friedman, Olivia Hom, Kelly Jiang, Anne Liu, Keiji Lohier, Rozalia Ostrowska, Maron Otndiola, Nathaniel Powers, Hui Qiong Rong, Cassandra Stevens, Zoe Woolrich, Grace Zhang, Tiffany Zhu

NYC Salt, New York
Teacher: Alexis Lambrou
Student: KeSean Taylor-Jack

Teacher: Emily Schiffer
Students: Isabel Abad-Munson, Elizabeth Avila, Benjamin Brown, Reveka Brown, Steven Chen, Max Cunningham, Makena Doran, Abigail Hammer, Alessia Hu, Maxie Krane, Andre Nikowitz, Heidi Perez, Daphne Tang, Emmersen Tormey, Violet Willoughby, Jason Yan, Morgan Ye, Irene Yachun Zhang, Nate Zim

Parkville High School, Baltimore
Teacher: Ariana Mygatt
Students: Evan Daniel, Ryan Dibley, Michael Feenster, Anthony Marchese,

Katherine Minaya, Larry Portillo Guzman, Hannah Pullifrone, Celine Ramirez, Suriya Santiago, Tayshaun Scott, Johanna Zea

Parole de photographes, École élémentaire Philippe de Girard, Paris
Teacher: Anita Pouchard Serra
Students: Nada Louisse, Courusisior Recei Manon, Alessandro Salazar Melendres, Evans Salazar Melendres

Phillips Academy, Andover, Massachusetts
Teacher: Hector René Membreno-Canales
Students: Kenichi Fujiwara, Zeena Kao, Ralph Lam, Nathalie Lelogeais, Kylie Lough

Project Kids & Cameras, Toronto
Teacher: Diana Nazareth
Students: Henry Ball, Alaya Coppard Murray, Carys Dosanjh, Ekam Dosanjh, Jackson Duffield, Madeleine Handson-Boyd, Simon Karmuells, Paulina Leyva-Arcos, Matt Maguire, Catalina Rodriguez Luna, Ruby Sabir

Project MiRa, Caracas, Venezuela
Teachers: Lexi Parra, Diko Betancourt
Students: Alesandra Cantos, Gabriela Cantos, Miguel Cardenas, Carlos Ernesto Centeno, Yarelis Gonzales, Oliver Gonzalez, Luisana Herrera, Nicole Longo, Manuel Martinez, Yilber Merchan, Yolmaryer Mora, Emily Paravaris, Levinson Prieto, Rachell Quintana, Rafael Quintana, Kelvim Requena, Jhoiner Rojas, Matías Rondón Pérez, Africa Rosas, Alicia Rosas Valero, Levi Seco, Rai Seco, Raul Urbina, Abril Villabolos Rojas

Queen Ethelburga's Collegiate, York, UK
Teacher: Megan Wellington-Barratt
Students: Abby Chen, Evgeniya Frolova, Sofya Glotova, Harvey Oldershaw, Katherine Sun

Rancho Buena Vista High School, Vista, California
Teacher: Kelly Clark
Students: Moises Aguilar, Amy Anderson, Amaya Andrews, Ashley Atempo, Harlie Blackstone, Christopher Boyd, Jose Calvillo, Leslie Cervantes, William Clarke, Elwin Cruz, Darrell Del Rosario, Kayla Durkes, Abigail Echevarria, Alma Galicia, Alicia Garcia, Aylin Gurrola, Miguel Heatherman, Adrianna Hernandez, Luis Hernandez, Vanessa Hernandez, Anabelle Huizar, Melvin Juarez, Hunter Krewson, Alexis Lopez, Lisa Lundberg, Megan Medrano, Ulisis Mejia, Emilie Morales, Luis Ortiz, Nathan Palos, Daniella Romero, Fabiola Ruiz, Aubrey Sierra

Reel Works, Mott Hall Bridges Academy, Brooklyn
Teachers: Liv Larsen, Hugo Rojas
Students: Mellisha Clarke, Kayla Ellison, Evangeline Garnes, Kahri Griffin, Kaila J., Vanessa L., Cassandra Larose, Preston Miller, Brandon Moore, Mijou Norman, Adeno Prescad, Amanda Williams, Trinity Williams, Eustacia Willis, Eve Willis

Srednja Šola za Oblikovanje in Fotografijo, Ljubljana, Slovenia
Teacher: Manca Juvan
Students: Nea Bekonjič, Jakob Blatnik, Neja Dulmin, Lana Grošelj, Ronja Jakomini, Timea Jelenovec, Kristina Klemenčič, Leon Kočevar, Manca Kompare, Daryna Kononenko, Klavdija Košir, Eva Kostadinov, Kaja Kristovič, Žiga Lupše, Lara Marušič, Ela Romih, Vesna Škofic, Ana Tomšič, Jan Vogrič

Stivers School for the Arts, Dayton, Ohio
Teacher: Leah Stahl
Students: Ayriel Brewster, Kaley Burden, Shawn Gardner, Robin Grigsby, Dakota Joy, Lillian Kizirnis, Olivia Koproski, Devin Lawrence, Andrew Leslie, Sandra Martinez, Nicole McBride, Mackenzie Moore, Julie Anne Moreland, Tatyanna Oglsby, Kennede Oninku, Olivia Patrick, Ruby Pobuda, Mea Richards, Ajaya Shelton, Anthony Thompson

Stsebetik Bolom, Chiapas, Mexico
Teacher: Maya Goded
Organizers: Margarita Martínez Pérez, Maruch Santíz
Students: Susana Petrona Pérez de la Torre, Karla Yumari Martínez Pérez

St. Vincent's Academy, Savannah, Georgia
Teacher: Carmela Aliffi
Teaching Assistants: Emma Hopson, Yi Lu
Students: Josephine Cetti, Lexi Dixon, Anna Giles Traux, Samantha Hargrove, Isabella Kelly, Anna Kropp, Ashley Lanier, Mary Sheffield, Rachel Steinfeldt

Through the Eyes of Children and BlinkNow, Surkhet, Nepal
Teachers: Jean Bizimana, Gadi Habumugisha, Mussa Uwitonze
Project Coordinator: Kristen Ashburn
Students: Shristi Aujhi, Mamata Bom, Swastika Dhaulakoti, Mina Giri, Hari Karki, Bipana Khadka, Puja Kumal, Shanti Nepali, Sundar Sunar

Through the Eyes of Children, Gisenyi, Rwanda
Teachers: Jean Bizimana, Gadi Habumugisha, Mussa Uwitonze
Project Coordinator: Kristen Ashburn
Students: Ayiragiye Denise, Dushime Olvier, Habumugisha Eric, Ineza Lisa, Iradukunda Mwajuma, Irumva Reponse, Mugisha Daniel, Mugisha Patrick, Muhawenimana Zawadi, Muhire Grite Olga, Mukashema Josine, Mushimiye Ariatha, Mushimiyimana Gisele, Nadiama Console, Ndarifite Blaise, Nishimwe Yvonne, Niyobuhungiro Aboubakar, Niyogisubizo Eritean, Niyogisubizo Heritier, Niyonsenga Clarisse, Niyonzima Didier, Ntwari Yan, Nyiranzamuhabwanimana Zawadi, Nzamukosha Angleque, Tuyisere Osama, Tuyishime Emmanuel, Uwamahoro Bebe, Uwimana Angelique, Yaraturagiye Gaudance

Transnational Villages Network/ Red de Pueblos Transnacionales (RPT), New York
Teacher: Cinthya Santos-Briones
Students: Heidy Animas, Angel Castillo, Kevin Diego, Michel Guadalupe Animas, Natalie Rodríguez, Emily Solano

Universidad Veracruzana Extension, Xalapa, Mexico
Teacher: Dolores Medel
Student: Frida Sofía Solano Morales

Visual Narratives Workshop, San Andrés Zautla, Mexico
Teacher: Octavio Lopez
Student: Jimena Lopez Garces

Waltham High School, Massachusetts
Teacher: Colleen Barber
Students: Anthony Galindo, Nilsen Hernandez Escalante, Kevin Rodriguez

William A. Shine Great Neck South High School, Great Neck, New York
Teacher: Lisa Stancati
Students: Gillian Aronov, Irena Cao, Victoria Cheng, Maggie DeMartin, Nadia Devereaux, Christopher Gee, Bradley He, Irene Hsu, Yunzhu Huang, Mingyue Hue, Sierra Hunter, Kiele Hwee, Emily Lee, Allison Liman, Benjamin Liu, Nicole Marinescu, David Meí, Derek Ng, Sabrina Ng, Corey Seng, Andrew Sheen, Victoria Song, Antonella Velaoras, Jonathan Wong, Wenjia Xia, Shiqi Xiao, Jenny Ye, Jinyeong Yu, Nancy Zhou

Young Photographers London
Teachers: Grace Gelder, Niaz Maleknia
Students: Rocco Grosso, Lucas Hetherton, Beth Hil, Jeanine Huang, Leah Camryn Jugoo, Romy McCarthy, Mylo Asher Mutongwizo, Karina Patel, Olivia Payne

YoVeoFoto, Barcelona
Teacher: Genia Valla
Students: Sofia Fernandez, Nikita Fesyuk, Lara Sofia Giacoman, Oleksander Tusko

Zentrum für Schulische und Psychosoziale Rehabilitation Westend, Berlin
Teacher: Jacobia Dahm
Students: Damla Ceylan, Kilian Dechering, Lukas Ernst, Dennis Forster, Jeremy Gerlach, Henning Hermann, Joelma Köhn-Bengui, Julian Krupka, Tessa Kuschinski, Paris Leitterstorf, Kim-Joeline Pewestorf, Ben Radszuweit, Amir Riahi, Leon Schulz, Jason Wallner, Victoria Werdnik, Lea Wilfarth, Melissa Wilhelm

Friends and family who submitted:
Carmen and Gustavo Gregg Rodriguez, Boston; Kate Ruwe, Hampstead, North Carolina; Abbey Ellerglick, Charlottesville, Virginia; Clementine Lang, San Francisco; January and William Murray, Brooklyn; Bahozhoni Tso, Flagstaff, Arizona; Noble and Prayer Young-Blackgoat, Flagstaff, Arizona

Eyes Open:
23 Photography Projects for Curious Kids
by Susan Meiselas

Cover: Zac Fay, *Buddies*, 2020

Editor: Denise Wolff
Designer: Atelier Dyakova, London
Senior Production Manager: True Sims
Production Manager: Andrea Chlad
Senior Text Editor: Susan Ciccotti
Copy Editor: Elena Goukassian
Editorial Assistant: Lanah Swindle
Work Scholars: Bowen Fernie, Joanna
Knutsen, Djuna Schamus, Arnold Barretto

Additional staff of the Aperture book
program includes:
Chris Boot, Executive Director; Lesley A.
Martin, Creative Director; Taia Kwinter,
Publishing Manager; Emily Patten, Publishing
Assistant; Samantha Marlow, Associate
Editor; Brian Berding, Designer; Kellie
McLaughlin, Chief Sales and Marketing
Officer; Richard Gregg, Sales Director, Books

Special thanks:
Eyes Open was made possible, in part, with
generous support from Jim Chervenak.
Additional thanks to the William Talbott
Hillman Foundation/The Affirmation Arts
Fund for their support.

First edition, 2020
Printed in China
10 9 8 7 6 5 4 3 2 1

Library of Congress Control Number:
2020909639
ISBN 978-1-59711-469-1

To order Aperture books, or inquire about
gift or group orders, contact:
+1 212.946.7154
orders@aperture.org

For information about Aperture trade
distribution worldwide, visit:
aperture.org/distribution

aperture

Aperture Foundation
548 West 28th Street, 4th Floor
New York, NY 10001
aperture.org

Aperture, a not-for-profit foundation,
connects the photo community and
its audiences with the most inspiring work,
the sharpest ideas, and with each other—
in print, in person, and online.